MW01095091

STRANGE
~BUT (MOSTLY) TRUE~
STORIES

--- BOOK 1 ---

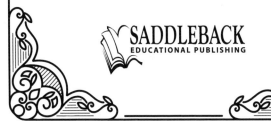

SADDLEBACK
EDUCATIONAL PUBLISHING

STRANGE
~BUT (MOSTLY) TRUE~
STORIES

SADDLEBACK
EDUCATIONAL PUBLISHING
www.sdlback.com

ISBN: 978-1-68021-701-8
eBook: 978-1-64598-070-4

Printed in Malaysia
26 25 24 23 22   3 4 5 6 7

TABLE OF CONTENTS

SAILING STONES

Can a 700-pound rock move along a flat surface by itself?

That is the mystery of a place called Racetrack Playa. This is in California. The large, flat area is part of Death Valley National Park. It was once a lake. But the water dried up long ago. Now, rocks of all shapes and sizes seem to slide across the land by themselves. These rocks, also called sailing stones, are clearly on the move. They leave long trails in the dirt behind them. Some are over 800 feet long. How is this possible?

Some people think the sailing stones are pushed by the wind. It is true that there are very strong winds in the area. However, not everyone agrees with this explanation. The rocks are very heavy. One study showed that it would take 500 mile-per-hour winds to move them. Winds that strong have never been recorded anywhere on Earth.

Another theory is that the rocks move when the ground becomes slippery. This happens after it rains. However, rain is rare. Only about two inches falls in the area each year. The stones move all the time. It seems that the weather does not matter.

There is another mystery. The rocks don't always move in a straight line. Sometimes they zigzag. Other times they turn and change directions. Plus, not all the stones move in the same direction at the same time.

It gets even weirder. The sailing stones have been studied since the 1940s. That is more than 70 years. Still, no one saw them move until 2013. Scientists took a series of pictures over a period of time. In them, the rocks could be seen making their way across the land.

Scientists studied the pictures carefully. They looked at the weather during the time they were taken. Rain had fallen in the area. When this happens, runoff from the surrounding mountains covers the dry lakebed. Temperatures then dropped. The shallow layer of water froze. It melted a little the next day and began to break up. Wind pushed the ice across the water. This slowly pushed the rocks forward. Sure enough, trails were left behind them.

Has the mystery of the sailing stones been solved? Many think so. But others are not quite ready to believe it.

THE STRANGE TRUTH

- Some people believe aliens move the rocks in Racetrack Playa. Others have said it is just people playing tricks.

- Winds blow across Racetrack Playa from the southwest to the northeast. This is the same direction many of the rocks move in.

- Sometimes the rocks can sit for over ten years without moving.

- When scientists observed the rocks moving in 2013, the water covering the lakebed was only three inches deep.

- Scientists say people may have seen the rocks moving before 2013 without realizing it. It would be hard to tell if one stone was moving if all of those around it were moving too.

DEATH BY MOLASSES

In 1915, a huge tank was built in Boston's North End. This was a busy shipping area on the harbor. From there, goods could easily be moved on and off ships. The steel tank was 50 feet tall and 90 feet wide. It was built to hold 2.5 million gallons of molasses.

Molasses was in high demand at the time. World War I was going on. The sweet, sticky liquid could be made into alcohol. Weapons factories then used this to make explosives. This alcohol was also used to make rum. Companies wanted to make as much rum as they could. Prohibition was starting soon. When Prohibition became law, their production would be shut down.

Many worried about the tank. It made noises all the time. There were several reasons. One was that it had been built in a hurry. Another was that the man in charge was not an engineer. He worked in finances. Safety measures were often overlooked. The steel walls of the tank were too thin. Plus, the rivets were not handled properly. Small cracks may have been made. From day one, the tank leaked. In fact, it was once painted brown. This was done to hide the leaks.

In mid-January 1919, the tank was topped off. It was filled with 2.3 million gallons of molasses. Two days later, disaster struck.

It was just after noon on January 15. People in the North End heard a low rumble. Then there were loud popping noises. It sounded like gunfire. The giant tank was bursting apart.

Suddenly, a wave of hot molasses gushed out. It was over 25 feet high. Buildings were smashed. A firehouse was knocked off its foundation. Steel support beams for an elevated train snapped in half. People were swept away and drowned. Horses were too.

The molasses spread over two city blocks. As it cooled, it slowed and thickened. This created more problems. It became harder for people and animals to move. In some places, the sticky goo was waist deep.

Rescuers worked for days. Cleanup efforts took even longer. The water in Boston Harbor was brown for months. In all, 21 people died in the flood. Over 150 were seriously injured. Many animals were also killed.

The tank was never rebuilt. For a long time after the flood, people could still smell molasses. This happened often on hot days.

THE STRANGE TRUTH

• Just before the disaster, the tank was filled with enough molasses to fill three and half Olympic-size swimming pools. It weighed 26 million pounds.

• The tank leaked constantly. Children would often fill cups with molasses that dripped out.

• The wave of molasses started out moving at 35 miles per hour.

• Some engineers today think the tank may have actually been designed to hold water, not molasses.

• The molasses flood caused over $7 million in property damage. Today, that is equal to over $100 million.

A HOLE IN THE HEAD

Construction jobs have many dangers. But rules keep workers fairly safe. One rule is that hard hats must always be worn. These protect the workers' heads. Still, accidents happen. Just ask Eduardo Leite.

In August 2012, the 24-year-old construction worker was on a job site. He and his crewmates were working on a tall building. It was a day like any other. Then a freak accident occurred.

An iron pole fell from five stories above. Leite was standing in the way. He had his hard hat on. But that did not matter. The six-foot pole went right through. It pierced the top of Leite's skull. Then it came out between his eyes.

Leite was rushed to a nearby hospital. He remained conscious and was able to tell doctors what happened. According to Leite's wife, he was not in much pain. The pole stayed in place the whole time.

Doctors decided to operate. They carefully cut open Leite's skull. The pole had gone through his brain. Pulling it out the front would be best. Five hours later, the surgery was complete.

Eduardo Leite was a very lucky man. Even after the operation, he felt little pain. Doctors were amazed. They said Leite had come close to losing an eye. He could have easily been paralyzed too. The pole was centimeters away from doing horrible damage.

How had Leite survive this freak accident? One doctor gave an explanation. He said the pole entered a "non-eloquent" part of the brain. This means it does not do anything specific or of great importance.

Leite had a quick recovery time too. Just a few weeks later, he left the hospital.

THE STRANGE TRUTH

- Leite appeared to have few lasting effects after the pole pierced his skull.

- In 1848, Phineas Gage was building a railroad. An accidental explosion shot a six-foot metal rod through his cheek and out the top of his head.

- Unlike Leite, Gage experienced big personality changes after his accident. He died 20 years later.

- The iron pole went through the right side of Leite's brain. This region is responsible for understanding emotions, recognizing danger, and noting the unfamiliar.

- Horrifying accidents such as Leite's and Gage's give doctors and scientists a chance to learn new things about the human brain.

THE MIRACLE GIRL

It was July 25, 1956. An ocean liner had recently left Italy for New York. It was called the *Andrea Doria*. There were several famous people on board. One passenger was 14-year-old Linda Morgan. She was not famous—yet.

After dinner, Morgan went to bed. While she slept, the *Andrea Doria* sailed into disaster.

People said the *Andrea Doria* was the safest ship ever. It had many safety features. There were watertight compartments and fireproof walls. These divided the ship into three zones. The 16 lifeboats could hold all of the ship's passengers. They even had room to spare.

The *Andrea Doria* was also known for its beauty and luxury. There were libraries and gyms. Areas were set aside for movies and dancing too. The ship was richly decorated.

Murals and tapestries covered the walls. It also had the latest technology. This included air conditioning.

Around 11:00 p.m., the crew saw something on the radar. Another ship was approaching. It appeared to be several miles away. The other ship was a Swedish ocean liner called the *Stockholm*. Its crew had also noticed the *Andrea Doria*.

An officer on the *Stockholm* looked through his binoculars. Somehow, the other ship was right in front of them. He yelled for the *Stockholm* to turn sharply. The *Andrea Doria* made a quick turn too.

Then the unthinkable happened. The *Stockholm* rammed right into the *Andrea Doria*.

Built for breaking up ice, the bow of the *Stockholm* was strong. It easily sliced through the side of the *Andrea Doria*. Water poured in, and the ship rolled over. Lights flickered. Then they went out. Frightened passengers ran through the dark passageways.

Both ships sent distress signals. Other boats raced to help. The *Stockholm*'s crew helped rescue 1,660 people off the *Andrea Doria*. In total, 51 people died. This included five passengers on the *Stockholm*.

Later, the *Stockholm*'s crew checked their ship for damage. Bernabé García was inspecting the bow. It was covered with pieces from the *Andrea Doria*. Suddenly, he heard a cry for help. García made his way through the wreckage. There, he found Linda Morgan.

García went to the girl. "Where am I?" she asked. "What ship is this?"

The crew of the *Stockholm* checked its passenger list. Morgan's name was not there. How had she ended up on the *Stockholm*'s bow?

It took a while to figure out. What happened was quite strange. The bow of the *Stockholm* rammed into the *Andrea Doria*. It hit just below Morgan's bed. Then the *Stockholm* pulled back. Young Morgan and her bed went with it.

Morgan had some injuries. But she was alive. She was eventually taken to a hospital in New York. Her biological father visited her there. He touched her cheek and smiled. "It is a miracle," he said. Linda Morgan's amazing story was soon in the news. Many were calling her "the miracle girl."

THE STRANGE TRUTH

- It is still unclear which ship's crew read their radar incorrectly before the collision.

- Morgan and her family were headed to New York for a vacation. Her sister and stepfather were killed in the accident. Her mother was badly injured.

- Morgan's injuries kept her in the hospital for months after the collision.

- Today, the *Andrea Doria* rests beneath 240 feet of water in the Atlantic Ocean. Diving conditions near the wreck are poor. More than 12 divers have died while exploring the shipwreck since 1956.

- Despite the ship accident, Linda Morgan does not have a fear of boats or the water. She has even been on several cruises. "It couldn't happen again," she once said.

THE BERMUDA TRIANGLE

The Bermuda Triangle is a very strange place. This area of ocean is bounded by Florida, Puerto Rico, and Bermuda. A number of ships and planes have disappeared there. Most of these vessels vanished without a trace. In many cases, there was no call for help. Searchers have never been able to find any survivors. Wreckage has not been found either.

One case is perhaps the most famous. It is the story of Flight 19.

It was December 5, 1945. World War II had ended just a few months earlier. Five bomber planes left Fort Lauderdale Naval Air Station. They carried 14 men on a practice bombing run. Their leader was Charles Taylor. Taylor was very experienced. He had 2,500 hours of flying time.

The bombers took off at 2:10 p.m. At 3:40 p.m., Taylor radioed in. He was lost. His compass did not seem to be working. Taylor thought he was flying over the Florida Keys. To reach the mainland, he decided to fly north. This was a bad idea. Flight 19 headed farther out to sea.

Two hours later, an air station located the planes. There was not a strong enough signal to radio directions. Meanwhile, the weather was getting bad. The five bombers were also running low on fuel.

Taylor radioed the other planes. "When the first plane gets down to ten gallons of gas, we'll land in the water together. Do you all understand?"

The air station heard one last radio call from Taylor. But the signal was weak. They could not understand his message.

Several search planes were sent to look for Flight 19. Shortly after takeoff, one of them disappeared. A ship reported seeing an explosion. Many believe this was the search plane.

A huge search began the next day. Over 300 planes and boats took part. They covered over 300,000 square miles. No one found a trace of Flight 19.

THE STRANGE TRUTH

* Some people think Flight 19 was abducted by aliens. But there are more logical explanations.

* The Gulf Stream in the triangle area moves very fast. Wreckage from planes and ships can easily be swept away.

* The ocean floor in the Bermuda Triangle features some of the deepest trenches in the world. Buried deep in a trench, a wrecked plane or ship would be very hard to find.

* Storms can develop very quickly in the triangle area. A ship or plane may not have time to call for help.

* The Bermuda Triangle is also called the "Devil's Triangle." A similar place exists off the east coast of Japan. It is called the "Devil's Sea." Many ships and planes have disappeared there too.

A WILD RIDE

A steeplechase is type of horse race. It is tough and dangerous. Jockeys ride horses around a course. They must jump over fences. Hedges and ditches must also be cleared.

During one memorable steeplechase, a horse fell. This is not unusual. But a moment later, something truly unbelievable happened.

This amazing race took place in 1953. It was held at England's famous Southwell Racecourse. Tim Molony rode a horse named Royal Student. Mick Morrissey rode Knother.

At the fifth fence, Royal Student was in the lead. Knother raced up behind him. Suddenly, Royal Student crashed. Molony was thrown to the ground. Unable to stop, Knother slammed into the fallen horse. Morrissey flew high into the air.

Royal Student struggled to his feet. Just then, Morrissey landed in the horse's saddle. He slowly rode Royal Student across the finish line. They finished in last place. But that didn't matter. Nobody at the track that day will ever forget the legendary event. Morrissey started the race on one horse and finished on another.

THE STRANGE TRUTH

- Royal Student was the top horse in the race that day. He was expected to win.

- Knother's odds of winning the race were 1 in 20.

- Mick Morrissey and Tim Molony were both jockeys from Ireland.

- Morrissey moved from one horse to the other without ever touching the ground.

- Morrissey and Royal Student walked the final two miles of the course to the finish line.

SEEING THE FUTURE

Jeane Dixon was America's most famous psychic. She was known for writing horoscopes. They were printed in hundreds of newspapers. Millions read them. Thousands sent her letters each week.

Dixon also made other predictions. The most famous one came in 1952. As the psychic tells it, she had a vision. There was a tall young man. He had brown hair. His eyes were blue. This man would become president in 1960. While in office, he would die.

Parade magazine printed Dixon's prediction in 1956. Four years later, John F. Kennedy was elected president. His description matched that of the man in the vision.

On November 22, 1963, Dixon was in Washington, D.C. She was having lunch with friends. Suddenly, she became upset. The psychic turned to her friends. "Something horrible is going to happen to the president today."

The news came just hours later. President Kennedy had been shot.

Dixon was already well-known. But with the prediction of Kennedy's death, her fame grew. She was invited to many parties. There, Dixon would give palm readings. A crystal ball was used to tell fortunes too. The psychic was asked to speak at events and on TV. Soon there were two best-selling books about her.

Born in 1918, Dixon was the child of German immigrants. As a young girl, she visited a fortune teller. The fortune teller saw that Dixon was a fellow psychic. She gave her a crystal ball. Dixon kept this gift for many years.

Another childhood story concerns Dixon's grandfather. One day she asked her mother about a letter. It had black edges. Her mother was confused. Nothing like that had been delivered. A few days later, a letter arrived. The edges were black. Sad news was written inside. Dixon's grandfather had died.

During World War II, Dixon read the fortunes

of servicemen. Soon she was getting tons of mail. Others wanted to know their futures too.

In 1944, President Franklin D. Roosevelt reached out. He invited Dixon to the White House. How long did he have to finish his work? Dixon answered gently. "Less than six months," she said. Roosevelt died three months later.

More of Dixon's predictions came true. The assassination of Martin Luther King Jr. was one of her visions. Dixon foresaw the 1964 Alaska earthquake. She also told of the fall of the Berlin Wall. Celebrity deaths were predicted too, including Marilyn Monroe's suicide.

Still, many of her predictions did not come true. World War III did not start in 1958. The Soviet Union did not put the first man on the moon. President George H. W. Bush was also not re-elected. Dixon explained the mistakes. She said the signs had not been read correctly.

Astrology helped Dixon make her predictions. Dreams, mind reading, and "inner voices" were used too. The psychic once described having a vision. "I feel that I am looking down from above . . . wondering why others cannot see what I am seeing." She also felt peacefulness and love.

Over time, Dixon's popularity faded. Newspapers stopped running the horoscopes. Many people thought the psychic was crazy. Some said she had only one skill. It was to make herself rich and famous.

But Dixon never took money for predictions. Her gift would be lost if she did. That is what Dixon believed. Helping others was always the focus. Meals were cooked for the blind and elderly. Troubled youths were invited to stay in her home. She also took in stray dogs and cats.

Jeane Dixon died of a heart attack at age 79. Had her own death been predicted? If so, she never said it out loud.

THE STRANGE TRUTH

• In 1977, Dixon met with Oprah Winfrey. She predicted that Oprah would have millions of fans and a big career.

• The "Jeane Dixon effect" is a term used to describe how people play up rare correct predictions while ignoring the many predictions that proved wrong.

• Dixon used a crystal ball but thought tarot cards and Ouija boards were evil.

THE DEAD MAN'S JOURNEY

Charles Coghlan grew up in the mid-1800s. His family wanted him to study law. But Coghlan wanted to perform. He began acting at age 17.

At first, Coghlan only had small parts in London theaters. In 1876, he went to the U.S. There, the actor found work on Broadway. Soon he was landing lead roles. Coghlan wrote his own plays too. Success brought him fame and fortune.

Eventually, Coghlan bought a farm in Canada. It was on Prince Edward Island. The farm became his summer home. He also hoped to retire there.

One day, the actor went to a fortune teller. She made a prediction. Coghlan would die in the southern part of the U.S. It would happen at the height of his career. His spirit would not rest until he returned home.

In 1899, Coghlan was in Galveston, Texas. This city is on the southern coast of the U.S. Coghlan was supposed to act in one of his own plays. But he came down with a bad stomach illness. Another actor played the part instead. Two days later, Coghlan had a heart attack and died. He was only 57 years old.

The actor's body was put in a metal coffin. His family members argued about where to bury it. Some hoped for Prince Edward Island. Others wanted France or London. That was where Coghlan grew up. While his family fought, Coghlan's coffin was buried in Galveston. It stayed there for almost a year.

On September 8, 1900, a powerful hurricane hit. There were strong winds and huge waves. Homes were smashed. Many people died. The storm destroyed Galveston. Even coffins were unearthed. Coghlan's was one of them.

Many of the washed-away bodies were found. They were reburied. But Coghlan's coffin was still missing. His family offered a reward to whomever found it.

It turns out Coghlan's body was on a journey. First, his coffin floated into the Gulf of Mexico.

Then it sailed around Florida. Next it headed up the coast of the U.S. In October 1908, a startling discovery was made. Coghlan's coffin was seen floating near Prince Edward Island. This was ten years after his death.

Finally, Coghlan had come home. His spirit could finally rest. The fortune teller's predictions seemed to have come true.

Did Coghlan's coffin really travel 2,000 miles from Texas to Canada? Some people think so. Others do not. Perhaps we will never know.

THE STRANGE TRUTH

- Prince Edward Island is located off the coast of eastern Canada.

- The Galveston hurricane of 1900 is considered one of the worst natural disasters in U.S. history. As many as 12,000 people may have died.

- Some newspapers said Coghlan's coffin was found in 1904 near Galveston. Others said it was found there in 1907. It was also reported that Coghlan's body was sent away before the hurricane hit.

- *Ripley's Believe It or Not* first reported Coghlan's traveling coffin story in 1927.

THE BIGHORN MEDICINE WHEEL

High in the mountains of Wyoming lies an ancient "wheel." This is called the Bighorn Medicine Wheel. Stones form its rim. They make up its center too. There are 28 stone spokes. Around the rim are six piles of rocks. These are shaped like rings. The wheel is huge. It is 80 feet across.

Similar medicine wheels have been found in Canada. Others dot the Great Plains in the U.S. There are some in Arizona too. The Bighorn Medicine Wheel is the best preserved. Who made these stone wheels, and why?

The Bighorn Medicine Wheel may give clues. It was built by Native Americans. Certain rock piles mark calendar dates. One is the summer solstice. This is the longest day of the year. On this morning, the sun rises over one of the rock piles. A second pile marks the sunset of that day. Other rock piles note when certain stars appear. These dates mark changes in seasons. All the wheels were built on high ground. That gives a clear view of the horizon.

Snow often covers the Bighorn Medicine Wheel. This is because it is high in the mountains. It can only be reached for two months a year. These are in midsummer. The wheel may have told Native Americans when to leave the mountain. They would not have wanted to get stuck in the snow. Native Americans may have also used the wheel in certain ceremonies.

Other large stone structures are found around the world. These are called megaliths. Some believe the stone wheels are like these. Their uses have changed over time. Stone wheels may have been used as burial sites or to mark special dates. They may also point to other wheels.

Some Native Americans still use the Bighorn Medicine Wheel. But why exactly was it built? No one knows for sure. Maybe we never will.

THE BIGHORN MEDICINE WHEEL

THE STRANGE TRUTH

◆ The Bighorn Medicine Wheel is located at the top of Medicine Mountain, part of the Bighorn Range in Wyoming.

◆ Medicine wheels may have been used in healing ceremonies. "Medicine," however, does not refer to the drugs we take to make us feel better. Native Americans believed the root of many sicknesses was spiritual.

◆ The Bighorn Medicine Wheel still predicts the summer solstice accurately.

◆ The oldest known medicine wheel is believed to be over 5,000 years old. It is found in Alberta, Canada.

◆ Scientists think the Bighorn Medicine Wheel is between 300 and 800 years old.

A DEADLY UMBRELLA

Georgi Markov was a Bulgarian who lived in England. He did not like the Bulgarian government. Markov often spoke out against it on radio shows. As a result, he had made some powerful enemies.

One day in September 1978, Markov was heading home from work. He waited at a bus stop. Suddenly, there was a sharp pain in his leg. Markov looked around. A man next to him was picking up an umbrella. "Sorry," the man said. Then the stranger jumped into a taxi and sped away.

Markov soon developed a high fever. He became very sick. Four days later, he died. The cause was blood poisoning.

Doctors examined Markov's body. They discovered a small pellet in his leg. Inside the pellet was ricin. This is a deadly poison. One tiny dose is enough to kill. How did it get in Markov's leg?

It was later found that Markov had been murdered. A Bulgarian secret service agent had carried out the attack. Many believe the umbrella at the bus stop was the murder weapon. It may have been rigged as a pellet gun. Others think a special pen was used. It could have injected the pellet into Markov's leg. The umbrella may have been dropped as a distraction.

THE STRANGE TRUTH

- Ricin is a natural poison found in the seeds of castor bean plants. It is one of the deadliest natural poisons.

- The pellet Markov was shot with was about the size of a pin head.

- The pellet that shot Markov held just 0.2 milligrams of ricin.

- There is no antidote for ricin poisoning.

- Scientists are exploring ways to use ricin as a cancer treatment.

SOLDIERS WHO WOULD
NOT SURRENDER

World War II ended in 1945. Soldiers around the world could put down their weapons. It was finally time to go home.

But not all soldiers were ready. Some did not believe the war was really over. Lieutenant Hiroo Onoda was one of them.

In 1942, Onoda joined the Japanese Army. Two years later, he was sent to the Philippines. He and his men were told to blow up a pier. Next, they needed to destroy an airfield. These plans were soon put aside.

American forces took over the island in February 1945. The Japanese Army withdrew. But Onoda was given orders to stay and fight. No matter what, he was not to surrender. His commanding officer made a promise. "It may take three years. It may take five. Whatever happens, we'll come back for you."

Onoda hid on the island with three other soldiers. They rationed their supplies. Using guerrilla warfare, they were able to survive.

In October 1945, the soldiers found a leaflet. It said the war had ended. But Onoda did not believe it. He and his men continued to hide.

Civilians on the island were fed up. They were no longer at war. But soldiers still hid in the jungle. These men shot at and stole from them. More leaflets were dropped by planes. Photographs and letters from relatives were too. Everything said the war was over. Japanese officials even shouted the news into the jungle using loudspeakers. Onoda and his men remained suspicious.

In 1949, one soldier finally surrendered. Another was killed in 1954. Two soldiers were left. One was Onoda. The other was a man named Kozuka. They lived in the jungle for another 20 years. Their job was to gather information about the enemy. This is what they believed. They waited for Japanese troops to return.

After 27 years in hiding, Kozuka was killed. This was in October 1972. Onoda was on his own.

Norio Suzuki was a Japanese college student. In 1974, he told his friends he was going to the Philippines. Suzuki joked about finding Onoda. Amazingly, he did.

Suzuki told Onoda that World War II was really over. The lieutenant was still not convinced. Onoda said he would only surrender if his commander ordered him to.

Now Suzuki had a new mission. He returned to Japan. A search led him to the elderly commander. His name was Major Taniguchi. Taniguchi traveled to the Philippines. There, he met with Onoda.

Taniguchi gave Onoda orders. All combat activity had to stop. The war was over. It was time to surrender. Onoda was shocked. He had spent 29 years fighting an imaginary war. That made him very angry.

Other Japanese soldiers hid out in the Philippines too. Onoda and his men were not the only ones. In 1972, Shoichi Yokoi surrendered. He was on the island of Guam. In 1974, another man surrendered on Morotai. This is an island in Indonesia. His name was Teruo Nakamura.

A group of 31 soldiers made it to the island of Anatahan. These men were from three Japanese ships that had been sunk. On the island, they lived simple lives. Their huts were built from palm fronds. They ate coconuts, fish, and even lizards.

One day, an American bomber crashed on the island. Its entire crew was killed. The Japanese soldiers took apart the plane. They used the scrap to make pots and knives. Metal roofs were placed on their huts. Parachutes became clothing.

People on a nearby island later discovered the Japanese soldiers. Pamphlets were dropped. They said that the war was over. But these were ignored.

Then, letters were dropped over the island. Japanese officials wrote them. Family members of the soldiers wrote some too. Finally, in June 1951, the group surrendered.

THE STRANGE TRUTH

- Guerrilla warfare is a type of armed conflict in which small groups make quick attacks on larger armies. These groups often consist of people who do not belong to an army themselves. They may be considered rebels.

- Onoda and his men killed around 30 civilians after World War II ended. They believed these people were their enemies. The president of the Philippines later forgave Onoda for these crimes.

- Onoda returned to Japan after being away for 29 years. The country was nothing like he remembered.

- Hiroo Onoda hid from search parties for years. He was declared dead in 1959. In reality, Onoda died in a Japanese hospital in 2014. He was 91 years old.

- A woman named Kazuko lived on Anahatan with her husband. She was the only woman on the island. Kazuko acted as a queen to the Japanese soldiers who hid there.

THE ROSWELL MYSTERY

It was the first week of July 1947. Something flew across the sky near the town of Roswell, New Mexico. Then it crashed. To this day, people disagree about what the object was. Some say it was a weather balloon. Others believe a flying saucer fell to Earth.

Mac Brazel was a rancher. The night of the sighting, he heard an explosion. He did not think much of it. It was a stormy night. Brazel went out to herd sheep the next day. That was when he found the wreck.

Strange debris was all over the field. There were sticks and rubber strips. Pieces of tough paper were scattered around too. Brazel brought some of the debris to a neighbor. The men tried to cut and burn the material. But they could not even make a mark.

"It was different from anything we'd ever seen," Brazel said. "Some of the material was like tinfoil. But when it was crushed, it would flatten itself out." On another piece, there were purple-pink figures. They reminded Brazel of writing. However, he had never seen the language before.

Brazel decided to report the wreck. He spoke with the Roswell sheriff. Then the sheriff called the Roswell Army Air Field. His neighbor's wife recalled the rancher being held at the Army base for a week. "Mac Brazel came back," she said. "But his story had changed. 'They say it was a weather balloon,' he said. And that's all he would say about it."

Frank Kaufmann worked at the air field. He remembered the crash too. "The radar screen lit up," he said. "Then calls started coming in. From people driving on highway 285. They said they'd seen a flame going down."

Kaufmann went to see base commander Colonel William Blanchard. A search party was formed.

"It was pitch black," Kaufmann said. "Off the highway, we could see a glow. The wreck did not look like a plane or a missile. Nothing like that. At least not from two to three hundred yards away. We radioed for the specialists—the chemical boys—to check out the area. They told us it was all right to go in. Then we got our first close look at the debris.

"We were dumbfounded. Didn't know what to think. How would people react if we told them what we saw. They'd probably think we were crazy."

Kaufmann claimed to have seen aliens at the crash site. "They were good-looking. Ash-colored faces and skin. About five feet four, five feet five. Small ears, small noses. Fine features. Hairless. There were five in all. I saw just two of them. One was thrown out of the craft itself. Another was half in and half out of the cabin. Did I mention they were all dead?

"I didn't go near the craft itself. I just took a quick look because we were so busy. Our job was to truck everything out of there before daylight. The craft was small. I'd say it must have been 20 to 22 feet long. Maybe 10 to 12 feet wide. Strangely, the craft carried no fuel.

"One of the men noticed that the aliens' skin

was falling apart. So we placed them in body bags. The bodies were the first to go, then the craft.

"It's something you live with all your life. You can't erase it from your mind. Seeing those bodies and seeing the craft—we're not alone."

The search team returned to the base. They were warned never to talk about the crash. Kaufmann said nothing about it until the 1990s. Then other witnesses also began talking about that strange event in 1947.

One of those witnesses was Glenn Dennis. Dennis worked at a funeral home in Roswell. He said a man from the Army base had called. The man asked about the availability of five child-sized caskets. Dennis asked the man what they were for. "We're just having a meeting here," the man said. "If we ever have an epidemic, we need to know what we have on hand."

Later that day, Dennis had to go to the base hospital. Noticing a number of ambulances parked outside, he peered in one of them. He saw something shiny. It looked like stainless steel. But there were strange purple, pink, and black shadings too.

Dennis entered the hospital. He needed someone to sign paperwork so he could get paid. While inside, he stopped in the hospital lounge for a drink. People in the area seemed tense.

"A captain was leaning in the doorway," Dennis recalled. "I said, 'Looks like you got a crash.' The captain wanted to know who I was. Then he ordered me off the base."

The next day Dennis met a friend in a coffee shop. This friend was an Army nurse from the hospital. She was upset and crying. According to the nurse, aliens had been brought to the hospital.

She drew a picture of the aliens on a napkin. They were small, with large heads and eyes. Each hand had four fingers. There were suction cups on the tips. A few days later, the nurse was transferred to England.

Dennis did not talk about the crash again until 1990. "Just didn't want to get involved. Never told my wife or anybody else. If I'd told this in 1947, who would have believed it anyway? I didn't want my kids getting made fun of because their dad saw flying things."

Walter Haut, a public information officer for the Army, was another witness. On July 7, 1947, he was asked to write a press release. It would announce that the Army had found a crashed flying saucer.

Haut delivered the press release to two newspapers and two radio stations. Soon the phones were ringing off the hook. Everyone wanted more information.

A few hours later, General Roger Ramey made another statement about the crash. In it, he stated that the found object was actually a weather balloon.

Haut never believed it.

In 1994, the Air Force issued a report about the crash. The report said that a weather balloon had indeed crashed near Roswell. But this was a top-secret spy balloon. Its purpose was to search the atmosphere for proof of Soviet nuclear tests.

In 1997, another report was released. This one was about the dead bodies of so-called aliens. The report said the "aliens" were really Air Force test dummies.

Even today, many people are not convinced. Some, like Mac Brazel's neighbor, say, "If we're here, why can't somebody else be out there?"

THE STRANGE TRUTH

♦ In its 1994 report, the Air Force said the weather balloon was part of a secret research project. It's code name was Project Mogul.

♦ Some Roswell Army Air Field officials worried that the wreckage was from a Russian satellite or spy plane.

♦ The events of early July 1947 are often referred to as the "Roswell incident."

♦ Sightings of unidentified flying objects (UFOs) have been reported for hundreds of years.

♦ Today, the town of Roswell celebrates the supposed 1947 alien crash with an annual UFO Festival. People from around the world attend the event.

WAS DRACULA REAL?

When people hear the word *vampire*, they often think of Dracula. There are many books and movies about him. His teeth are sharp and pointy. He bites someone's neck. Then the vampire drinks their blood. The sun burns him. That is why Dracula must hide until night.

Dracula is a made-up character. He first appeared in a book by Bram Stoker. Where did the author get the idea?

Vampire stories have been around for thousands of years. There are many legends. But the Dracula story is based on a *real* person. His name was Vlad III Dracula. He is also known as Vlad the Impaler.

Vlad was born in Transylvania in 1431. Today, Transylvania is part of Romania. The name Dracula comes from the Latin word *draco*. That means "dragon." *Dracula* means "son of the dragon." Vlad's father belonged to a special group. It was called the Order of the Dragon.

In 1436, Vlad's father became the prince of Walachia. This is also part of Romania. He was killed in 1447.

Vlad soon learned of his father's death. He set out to take back the throne. Between 1448 and 1476, he ruled several times.

During these years, Vlad became known for being evil. He would often impale his enemies on sharp stakes. They would be left there to die. These terrible acts earned him the name Tepes. This means "the impaler."

Vlad's life was filled with war. Legend says he impaled 20,000 people in one day. The field of bodies also served to scare his other enemies.

Some historians believe Vlad drank the blood of his victims. An old poem says the ruler would eat among the dead. He would also dip bread in their blood. But some say the original poem had a different meaning. It says Vlad washed his hands in blood before eating. Is this where the story of Dracula came from?

THE STRANGE TRUTH

- Vlad III Dracula was killed in 1476.

- Bram Stoker's book *Dracula* was first published in England in 1897.

- *Dracula* takes places in Transylvania, which is where Vlad the Impaler was born.

- In Romania, Vlad III is viewed as a national hero.

- Stoker might have had other inspiration for Dracula too. European folktales of the undead, Irish folklore, and other vampire fiction from around Stoker's time may have helped shape the character.

THE LAWN CHAIR PILOT

Larry Walters was 33 years old. For 20 years, the truck driver had dreamed of flying. On July 2, 1982, he finally did it. Walters strapped himself into a lawn chair. Then he zoomed into the sky.

Tied to the lawn chair were 42 large weather balloons. Each was filled with helium. This made the chair float. Several jugs of water were also attached. The weight of the water kept the chair steady. Walters packed little else. He brought a parachute, an altimeter, a CB radio, and a BB gun.

Walters' strange journey began outside his girlfriend's house. She lived in San Pedro, California. The lawn chair pilot took his seat. Then the ropes tying down the chair were cut.

"I took off so quickly, it knocked my glasses

off." Walters said. "I couldn't see very well. But I could tell I was going up fast."

In fact, Walters was traveling at 1,000 feet per minute. When he reached 16,000 feet, he was high enough. This was about three miles above the earth. To stop climbing, Walters shot a few balloons with the BB gun.

Pilots of TWA and Delta airplanes reported seeing Walters. One called in the strange sight. Walters was not supposed to be in federal airspace. He could get hit by a plane.

Walters hoped to reach the Rocky Mountains. But there was not enough wind to take him there. He was also getting very cold.

After almost two hours in the air, Walters wanted to get back to Earth. "I started shooting at the balloons. As each one popped, the chair would go a little lower. After a while, it was gliding over the tops of streets and buildings and houses. That was the scariest part. I was especially afraid my chair would hit the power lines. If that happened, I'd get electrocuted."

In fact, Walters did float under some power lines. The balloons got caught. He and his chair swung back and forth. That was enough for him.

Carefully, the pilot climbed out of his seat. Then he dropped safely to the ground.

His odd flight made Walters famous. He appeared on two late-night TV shows. The Smithsonian Institution even asked for his lawn chair. It wanted to put the chair on display. But Walters had given it away after landing.

Walters achieved his dream of flying. But it was not without consequences. His stunt had broken several laws. He had to pay a $1,500 fine to the Federal Aeronautics Agency. Still, Walters felt it was something that had to be done. "A man can't just sit around," he said.

THE STRANGE TRUTH

- An altimeter is a tool that measures altitude, or how high something is above sea level.

- It is estimated that Walters spent around $4,000 on supplies for his flight at an Army-Navy surplus store.

- Walters flew in his lawn chair for 21 miles.

- Walters had named his lawn chair "Inspiration I."

- Walters braved air temperatures as low as 5 degrees Fahrenheit.

DOUBLE LOTTERY WINNER

The chances of winning the lottery are not great. Winning twice is even more unlikely. Still, it happens more than many people would think.

Just ask Cary Collings. This Washington man won big, twice. His story is truly amazing.

Collings's first bit of luck came on June 14, 2013. He played "Red Hot 5s," a scratch-off lottery game. The ticket Collings bought was a winner. It was for the top prize—$55,555.

The next morning, Collings went to pick up his winnings. Feeling inspired, he decided to try his luck again. He bought three "Bring on the Bens" scratch-offs. Collings scratched the first ticket. It was a $200,000 winner.

In less than 24 hours, Collings had won

$255,555. His only plans for the money were to pay off some debts.

Winning the lottery multiple times is rare. However, it has happened to other people too.

British businessman George Traykov considers himself lucky. He won the lottery twice in two years. His winnings totaled $1.8 million.

Mary Riedel won $50,000 in the Ohio Lottery in 2014. She gave most of her winnings to her family. Four months later, Riedel purchased another lotto ticket. It was a winner. This time the prize was $100,000.

Mark Maltz is a truck driver from Michigan. In February 2018, he bought a scratch-off ticket. It was a $10 winner. Maltz decided to buy another. With the second scratch-off, he won $15. This money was used to buy two more tickets. On one of them, the truck driver won the grand prize. It was just over $325,000.

Winning the lottery is a dream for many. Imagine winning more than once. Are you feeling lucky?

THE STRANGE TRUTH

- The Mega Millions lottery prize reached over $1 billion for the first time in history in October 2018. A South Carolina resident won the jackpot, which was $1.5 billion.

- A Powerball ticket holder has a 1 in 292 million chance of winning the top prize.

- Are lottery winners cursed? The *New York Daily News* reported that 70 percent of them go broke within seven years of winning big.

- A lucky couple in Virginia won a $1 million lottery drawing in 2014. Two weeks later, they won another $50,000. The next day, they won $1 million on a scratch-off.

- In North America, the lottery is a $70 billion-a-year industry.

THE NIGHT MARCHERS

It is late at night. Lights are seen moving down a mountainside. These are the night marchers, or *huaka'i pō*. They are the spirits of ancient Hawaiian warriors. These warriors walk together in a ghostly procession.

Usually, the marchers are seen at night. Sometimes they cannot be seen at all. Still, they may be heard. The ghosts chant. There is music too. It is played on conch shells and drums.

Torches light the procession. A ghost at the front carries a spear. He will kill anyone in the marchers' way. It is his duty. His spear will bring immediate death.

A warning is called out. The living should get out of the way.

Ghost marchers might have living family members. They may watch the procession. If a ghost sees a relative, he will shout. This stops the spearman. He will not throw his spear at the heart of the watching relative.

This is an old Hawaiian legend. Legends are stories that are passed down. Older people tell them to younger generations. Some may be based in truth. But there is often no way to know what is fact and what is fiction.

A story is told about the night marchers. There was once an elderly Japanese man who was deaf. One night, he went fishing. People who lived near the beach heard the night marchers coming. They ran off. The elderly man heard nothing. By the time he saw the ghostly procession it was too late. The next morning, people found his body near the water. Doctors said the elderly man died of a heart attack. But some people are not so sure.

Turn and run if the night marchers appear. Do not cry out or look back. Try not to call attention to yourself. There may not be time to escape. If this happens, remove your clothes and lie down on the ground. Do not move or look up. Then just hope you do not get a spear through your back.

THE STRANGE TRUTH

- In Hawaii, scary stories that give you goose bumps—like ghost stories—are called "chicken skin" stories.

- When they were alive, the marchers' job was to protect sacred people such as chiefs. These people were so revered, commoners were not allowed to look at them. Anyone who did would be killed.

- To protect the lives of commoners, the marchers traveled by night. This meant there was less chance of someone seeing a chief and facing their death.

- The night marchers are often seen around sacred Hawaiian sites such as temples. They appear for several nights, just before a new moon. This is when the moon is completely dark.

- The night marchers were supposedly caught on a security camera in 2012. The cleaning woman who saw them died the next day. A month later, she was seen marching in their procession.

SOLDIER WITHOUT A GUN

Desmond Doss joined the Army in 1942. He wanted to serve his country in World War II. But Doss was very religious. Because of this, he refused to carry a gun.

At first, the Army had a problem with Doss's choice. The U.S. was at war. Soldiers needed guns. They provided protection. It seemed impossible not use one.

Still, Doss wanted to serve his country. He was placed with a rifle company. Many soldiers disliked this. They were mean to Doss. Some felt his refusal to carry a gun might get them killed.

Soon the situation changed. The Army recognized Doss's wishes. He was given a special status. Doss also would not work on Saturdays. It was his religion's holy day.

Doss became an Army medic. He would

run onto the battlefield to treat the wounded. Soldiers could have life-threatening injuries. Other times their wounds were minor. It did not matter. His own safety was put aside so he could help others.

As a medic, Doss helped those who had been mean to him. He believed in treating others the way you wanted to be treated.

By May 1945, the war was slowly winding down. Doss's division was in Japan. They were trying to capture a rocky cliff. The soldiers called this area Hacksaw Ridge. Japanese soldiers were fighting with everything they had. But the Americans eventually took control of the area.

The Japanese launched a final attack. American soldiers were not ready. An order to retreat was given. Many soldiers did not make it out. Some were killed. Others were severely wounded. This was when Doss sprang into action.

Doss ignored the order to retreat. He also put his religion aside. It was a Saturday, but he got to work. For 12 hours, he saved as many men as possible. Soldiers were dragged to the edge of the cliff. Then Doss lowered them to safety with a rope sling. The medic prayed the whole time.

That day, Doss saved 75 men. Many had been cruel to him during training. Several weeks later, Doss was injured in combat. A grenade blew up near his leg. Then he was shot in the arm. Amazingly, Doss survived.

In October 1945, Doss received a Medal of Honor. He was also given a Purple Heart and a Bronze Star. Doss never carried a gun in World War II. But he had been a brave hero.

THE STRANGE TRUTH

- The special status Doss was given was that of a conscientious objector. This is what people who refuse to carry weapons or serve in the armed forces based on their morals or religious beliefs are called.

- Doss's heroic story was the subject of the Academy Award–winning film *Hacksaw Ridge*.

- In 1946, Doss developed tuberculosis. His left lung had to be removed. He lived for over 50 years with just one lung.

- Doss estimated that he saved 50 lives at Hacksaw Ridge. His commanding officer gave him credit for saving 100. They came to an agreement that he saved 75 people that day.

KILLER LAKES

It was August 21, 1986. Ephriam Che was feeling uneasy. "Something is wrong," he told himself. He headed downhill toward the village. "It is very wrong."

Che lived in Africa. His mud-brick house sat on a cliff. Below was Lake Nyos. The lake was in a volcanic crater.

The night before, Che had heard a rumbling noise. It sounded like a rockslide. That had been around 9:00 p.m. He stepped outside. But it was too dark to see what was happening. All he could make out was a strange white mist rising from the lake. Che was healthy. Still, the young man felt sick as he got into bed.

In the morning, Che rushed to the village. He was eager to check on his family. The village was strangely quiet. Nobody was laughing or talking. Birds were not singing. Insects did not buzz. There was only silence. That is when Che knew. His hunch had been right. Something terrible had happened.

Silence was not the only warning. The lake usually sparkled blue. That day it was dull and red. There was also a waterfall. But it was dry.

The man panicked. He went to the center of the village. There, Che made a ghastly discovery. Almost every villager was dead. This included his whole family.

People were not the only victims. All the insects and animals in the area were dead too. Plants around the lake had been killed. Dead fish floated on top of the water.

Che thought the end of the world had come. "All I remember is crying," he said later.

———————————————

That day, nearly 1,800 people died around Lake Nyos. Two years earlier, 47 people died near Lake Monoun. This is another African crater lake. The lakes are only 60 miles apart. Perhaps all the deaths were related.

Scientists looked into the tragedy at Lake

Monoun. They found some important clues. The water in the lake was dangerous. It was loaded with carbon dioxide gas. Monoun had become a "killer lake."

Carbon dioxide gas is also called CO_2. It is what makes soda pop fizz. This gas has other uses too. Fire extinguishers are filled with it. CO_2 puts out fires by smothering them.

In small amounts, CO_2 is not harmful. But the water of Lake Nyos was saturated. The gas exploded out of the lake. This sucked the oxygen from the air. People and animals in the area could not breathe. They were basically smothered to death.

Killer lakes form naturally. CO_2 gas rises from a volcano underneath. The weight of the water traps the CO_2 at the bottom of the lake. Pressure increases as the water becomes filled with the gas. When it gets to be too much, the CO_2 bursts from the lake.

There is an easy way to think about this. Imagine shaking a bottle of soda. Pressure builds up inside. When the bottle is opened, the soda shoots out. This is similar to what happened at the killer lakes.

What caused the release of so much CO_2? Scientists are not sure. It may have been a rockslide. Strong winds or a temperature change could also be to blame. Whatever the reason, it could happen again soon. Tests showed the gas was quickly building up. The scientists had to act fast. They needed to prevent another tragedy.

Engineers began working on the problem. They finally figured it out. The gas needed to be drawn off the lake gradually. Pipes were installed. Now, small amounts of gas are able to rise through the pipes. Then it is released into the air above.

Still, not all problems with the killer lakes have been solved. For one thing, the cost of drawing off the gas is very high. Poor countries are not able to afford it. The U.S. stepped in to help pay for pipes at Lake Nyos.

Are there other killer lakes? It is very likely. But we may not discover them until it is too late.

THE STRANGE TRUTH

◆ Many of the people who died at Lake Nyos were found where they would usually be around 9:00 p.m. This suggests that they died instantly.

◆ After the gas explosion, some villagers who survived laid unconscious for over a day before waking up.

◆ At first, scientists thought the volcano beneath Lake Nyos had erupted. It took them many months to figure out what really happened.

◆ One scientist wrote a paper about the natural disaster that occurred at Lake Monoun. But other scientists rejected his idea that CO_2 had built up in the water and then exploded. They thought it was too unbelievable.

◆ Carbon dioxide is a colorless, odorless gas. This means it is difficult to detect, which makes it very dangerous. Air that is 30 percent CO_2 can kill people on the spot.

FIRE IN THE MINES

Centralia, Pennsylvania, was once a big coal mining town. One hundred years ago, 1,200 people lived there. Shops and homes lined the streets. As the demand for coal grew, the population jumped to 2,700. Coal drove the economy. It helped the town survive the Great Depression.

Today, Centralia looks very different. It is now a ghost town. Once-busy streets are empty. Few buildings remain standing. Smoke fills the air. In 2017, there were only seven people living there. The reason is both incredible and terrifying.

Three hundred feet underground, a fire burns. It started over 50 years ago. But how?

Trash was a big problem in Centralia. There were a number of unregulated dumps. They smelled bad and attracted rats. In 1962, a new landfill was opened. An old mine pit was filled with garbage from the dumps. Just before Memorial Day that year, the town decided to clean up the landfill. The easiest way was to burn the trash inside.

This seemed like a good idea. Then the flames spread. A nearby line of underground coal caught fire. Soon it moved into coal tunnels beneath the town. Attempts were made to put out the flames. But nothing worked. There were too many abandoned mine tunnels. It was impossible to know which ones needed to be closed off. Mines that were still in use filled with dangerous carbon monoxide gas. They were soon shut down.

The ground underneath Centralia became very hot. Some areas were over 900 degrees Fahrenheit. It was so hot, a match would light if held near the ground. Sinkholes began appearing. One caught a 12-year-old boy off guard in 1981. He barely made it out alive. Graves in two of the town's cemeteries were swallowed up. Many homes were destroyed. Centralia went up in smoke.

Eventually, Congress gave residents money to move. Despite the dangers, some people refused to leave. In 1992, all of the buildings in the town were condemned. Many were knocked down. Centralia's zip code was taken away in 2002. The few people who still live there are not allowed to sell their property. They cannot give it to family members eithers.

Someday, Centralia will be completely abandoned. For now, police try to keep out curious tourists. Dangers from the underground fires will continue for years to come.

THE STRANGE TRUTH

- Fire needs oxygen, fuel, and heat to burn. Mine tunnels bring oxygen down from the surface. Coal contains carbon, which acts as fuel. It burns slowly and steadily. This creates a lasting heat source. These conditions mean coal fires can burn for many years.

- Some of the largest coal deposits in the world are found in Central Pennsylvania.

- The fire in Centralia covers an eight-mile area and may burn for another 250 years.

- Thousands of mine fires burn around the world. The "Burning Mountain" fire in Australia has been burning for 6,000 years.

- In 2018, Centralia was one of 38 active mine fires known to be burning in Pennsylvania.